Penguin Books

CULTURE SHOCK

Most people ignore most poetry
because
Most poetry ignores most people.

If you've always thought this was true you're in for a shock, because Michael Rosen has uncovered a huge range of poetry, spaning different ages and cultures, which deals with the issues confronting all teenagers today. Love, hate, racism, sexism, poverty and peer pressure are some of the many different topics covered in this innovative anthology, where a mixture of poetry, graffiti, famous quotes, lyrics and epitaphs make a thought-provoking and very entertaining read.

With stunning illustrations by Andrzej Krauze and work from a diverse range of contributors including John Agard, Alice Walker, Stevie Smith, Adrian Mitchell, Marilyn Monroe, Monty Python, D. H. Lawrence, Attila the Stockbroker and Bertolt Brecht, this is an informal and accessible anthology that won't be ignored.

Michael Rosen is a writer, poet, performer and broadcaster, and script-writer and has been writing for children of all ages since 1970. Born in 1946, he lives in London with his wife and five children, spending his time writing, visiting schools, doing TV and radio programmes (including more recently presenting *Treasure Island* on Radio 4) and shopping. His books for Puffin include *Quick, Let's Get Out of Here*, *Wouldn't You Like to Know* and *You Can't Catch Me!* He has also worked with Roger McGough on *You Tell Me*.

CULTURE SHOCK

Edited by Michael Rosen

Illustrated by Andrzej Krauze

PENGUIN BOOKS

PENGUIN BOOKS

Published by the Penguin Group
Penguin Books Ltd, 27 Wrights Lane, London w8 5TZ, England
Viking Penguin, a division of Penguin Books USA Inc.
375 Hudson Street, New York, New York 10014, USA
Penguin Books Australia Ltd, Ringwood, Victoria, Australia
Penguin Books Canada Ltd, 2801 John Street, Markham, Ontario, Canada L3R 1B4
Penguin Books (NZ) Ltd, 182–190 Wairau Road, Auckland 10, New Zealand

Penguin Books Ltd, Registered Offices: Harmondsworth, Middlesex, England

First published by Viking Books 1990
Published in Penguin Books 1991
10 9 8 7 6 5 4 3 2

This selection copyright © Michael Rosen, 1990
Illustrations copyright © Andrzej Krauze, 1990
The Acknowledgements on page 109–113 constitute an extension of this copyright page.
All rights reserved

Filmset in 11/13pt Sabon

Printed in England by Clays Ltd, St Ives plc

Contents

Stereotype   *John Agard*   1

Here lies a poor woman who always was tired
   Catherine Alsopp   4

Prison Reform   *Pat Arrowsmith*   5

Radio Rap   *Attila the Stockbroker*   6

Note on Intellectuals   *W. H. Auden*   7

Girls Can We Educate We Dads?   *James Berry*   8

Harvest Hymn   *John Betjeman*   10

th guy drivin round in   *bill bisset*   12

The Democratic Judge   *Bertolt Brecht*   12

the longer i write poems for you   *Pamela Brown*   14

You want to change the world   *Dr Kit Bryson and
   Jean-Luc Legris*   14

There was a young lady named Bright   *Arthur Buller*   14

she had more friends   *Joanne Burns*   15

On Midas's Art   *Sir John Byrom*   16

Earwigs   *Raymond Carver*   17

Slickness   *Michael Casey*   19

Nostalgia   *Iain Chapman*   20

The trouble with some women   *Cher*   22

Reported Missing   *Barry Cole*   22

track suit   *John Cooper Clarke*   24

From June to December   *Wendy Cope*   26

Eat More   *Joe Corrie*   27

there are so many tictoc   *e. e. cummings*   28

War Memorials 1914–18   *Bob Dixon*   30

Here lies the mother of children seven
    J. S. Drennan   31

Madman   *Paul Durcan*   31

Broadminded   *Ray Durem*   32

The moon people   *William Eastlake*   33

Sho Nuff   *Nilene O. A. Foxworth*   34

Definition   *Erich Fried*   36

When asked his opinion of Western Civilization
    Mahatma Gandhi   36

Mr Jones   *Harry Graham*   37

He Had a Dream   *Sam Greenlee*   37

Three Poems for Women   *Susan Griffin*   38

Strange But True   *Mike Harding*   39

English Literature – GCE   *Savitri Hensman*   40

Impossibilities to His Friend   *Robert Herrick*   41

What is a Canary?   *Rita Ann Higgins*   42

Brief Reflection on Death   *Miroslav Holub*   44

Brief Thoughts on Maps   *Miroslav Holub*   44

i once addressed   *Keith Horn*   46

A weak-eyed adder known as Alf
    Wilbur G. Howcroft   46

50–50   *Langston Hughes*   47

Final Curve   *Langston Hughes*   48

Untitled   *Jeltje*   49

I'm starting to wonder   *Margaret Blair Johnstone*   49

JILL   I'm upset you are upset   *R. D. Laing*   49

DOCTOR   How are you?   *R. D. Laing*   50

Family Planning   *Fran Landsman*   51

Middle-Class Children   *D. H. Lawrence*   52

Tourists   *D. H. Lawrence*   54

Me Aunty Connie   *Terry Lee*   54

The sheep and the wolf   *Abraham Lincoln*   56

Pearls   *Jean Little*   57

Eve   *Kate Llewellyn*   58

Madam   *Christopher Logue*   60

Poem to Help Unemployment   *Liz Loxley*   61

Archy is Shocked   *Don Marquis*   62

Goodbye   *Carol-Anne Marsh*   64

Fire Guard   *Roger McGough*   68

Celia Celia   *Adrian Mitchell*   69

Most people ignore most poetry   *Adrian Mitchell*   69

Marilyn Monroe was once asked by a reporter   69

All Things Dull and Ugly   *Monty Python*   70

No Say   *Millie Murray*   72

My Black Triangle   *Grace Nichols*   74

Running Shoes (Guide to Technical Terms)   *Nigel*   75

Life & Trousers   *Andy P.*   76

By the time you swear you're his   *Dorothy Parker*   76

In America   *Tom Pickard*   76

Spic take the broom   *Pedro Pietri*   77

Evolution   *Fiona Pitt-Kethley*   78

Epigram   *Alexander Pope*   79

Better You Should Learn Wen Do
  Helen Potrebenko   79

The Starved Man   *Robert Priest*   80

Proverb from the Prophet of Palermo   81

Hustlers   *Cecil Rajendra*   82

Song of Bali   *W. S. Rendra*   83

Epitaph on Charles II   *John Wilmot,*
  Earl of Rochester   86

Lamentations   *Siegfried Sassoon*   86

Rodger   *Seething Wells*   87

Miriam   *Modesto Silva*   88

The Past   *Stevie Smith*   89

Two Old Women   *Anna 'Swir'*   89

Noise   *Steve Turner*   90

Bertha's Wish   *Judith Viorst*   91

Mississippi Winter IV   *Alice Walker*   91

I'm Really Very Fond   *Alice Walker*   92

Little Red Riding Hood   *Ania Walwicz*   93

Greatest Love of All   *Mbeke Waseme*   94

We Sat Talking   *Mbeke Waseme*   95

Who Wants to Know?   *Jim Wheat*   96

Classifieds   *Jim Wheat*   98

Here We Go   *Who Dares Wins Comedy Team*   99

Shelley Winters once revealed   100

Down With Fanatics!   *Roger Woddis*   100

Equal Opportunity   *Jim Wong-Chu*   102

Mirror Mirror   *Mitsuye Yamada*   104

Two Strings to a Bow   *Anon.*   104

How We Met   *By a fourth-year boy in a North
    London Comprehensive*   105

If all the trains at Clapham Jctn   *Anon.*   105

Here Lies Lester Moore   *Anon.*   106

Here lies the body of SAMUEL YOUNG   *Anon.*   106

Here lies my adviser, Dr Sim   *Anon.*   107

She lived with her husband 50 years   *Anon.*   107

To the Moon   *Anon.*   108

Acknowledgements   109
Index of First Lines   115

Stereotype

I'm a fullblooded
West Indian stereotype
See me straw hat?
Watch it good

I'm a fullblooded
West Indian stereotype
You ask
if I got riddum
in me blood
You going ask!
Man just beat de drum
and don't forget
to pour de rum

I'm a fullblooded
West Indian stereotype
You say
I suppose you can show
us the limbo, can't you?
How you know!
How you know!
You sure
you don't want me
sing you a calypso too
How about that

I'm a fullblooded
West Indian stereotype
You call me
happy-go-lucky
Yes that's me
dressing fancy
and chasing woman
if you think ah lie
bring yuh sister

I'm a fullblooded
West Indian stereotype
You wonder
where do you people
get such riddum
could it be the sunshine
My goodness
just listen to that steelband

Isn't there one thing
you forgot to ask
go on man ask   ask
This native will answer anything
How about cricket?
I suppose you're good at it?
Hear this man
good at it!
Put de willow
in me hand
and watch me stripe
de boundary

Yes I'm a fullblooded
West Indian stereotype

that's why I
graduated from Oxford University
with a degree
in anthropology

John Agard

In 1905, Catherine Alsopp, a Sheffield washerwoman, composed her own epitaph before hanging herself:

Here lies a poor woman who always was tired;
She lived in a house where help was not hired,
Her last words on earth were: 'Dear friends, I am going
Where washing ain't done, nor sweeping, nor sewing.
But everything there is exact to my wishes,
For where they don't eat, there's no washing of dishes
I'll be where loud anthems will always be ringing
But having no voice, I'll be clear of the singing.
Don't mourn for me now, don't mourn for me never,
I'm going to do nothing for ever and ever.'

Prison Reform

In the bad old days
no watches were permitted.
We did our time
not knowing what the time was.

Now watches are allowed
we have the satisfaction
of knowing how slowly
the time passes.

Pat Arrowsmith

Radio Rap

I turned on the radio this afternoon
with half a brain for a mindless tune
and if you want some mindless fun
it's always there on Radio One
The braincell level is very low
a diminished braincell ratio
and if your IQ's under five
it's just the stuff to keep you alive!
Synth pop and electrofunk
and endless hours of boring junk –
if that reflects the nation's taste
then this generation's gone to waste!
So where's the challenge? Where's the news?
Where's the ones who'll light the fuse?
Well I can see them all around
but they never make the D J sound
'cos the senile programmers get the bird
if they hear an idea or a naughty word
so all we get to pass the days
are boring endless pop clichés
LIKE
shake your booty on the floor
hang your wombat out the door
whomp that flounder, hit that plaice
wrap that turbot round my face

save your love 'cos the girl is mine
get on down, it's disco time
OK ya and I'm all right
the happy sound on a Saturday night
And then on top of that powerful stuff
if you didn't think that was rough enough
the daytime D Js cap the lot –
THEY SHOULD BE ROUNDED UP AND SHOT!

Attila the Stockbroker
(extract)

Note on Intellectuals

To the man-in-the-street, who, I'm sorry to say
    Is a keen observer of life,
The word Intellectual suggests straight away
    A man who's untrue to his wife.

W. H. Auden

Girls Can We Educate We Dads?

Listn the male chauvinist in mi dad –
a girl walkin night street mus be bad.
He dohn sey, the world's a free place
for a girl to keep her unmolested space.
Instead he sey – a girl is a girl.

He sey a girl walkin swingin hips about
call boys to look and shout.
He dohn sey, if a girl have style
she wahn to sey, look
I okay from top to foot.
Instead he sey – a girl is a girl.

Listn the male chauvinist in mi dad –
a girl too laughy-laughy look too glad-glad
jus like a girl too looky-looky roun
will get a pretty satan at her side.
He dohn sey – a girl full of go
dohn wahn stifle talent comin on show.
Instead he sey – a girl is a girl.

James Berry

Harvest Hymn

We spray the fields and scatter
    The poison on the ground
So that no wicked wild flowers
    Upon our farm be found.
We like whatever helps us
    To line our purse with pence;
The twenty-four-hour broiler-house
    And neat electric fence.

All concrete sheds around us
    And Jaguars in the yard,
The telly lounge and deep-freeze
    Are ours from working hard.

We fire the fields for harvest,
　The hedges swell the flame,
The oak trees and the cottages
　From which our fathers came.
We give no compensation,
　The earth is ours today,
And if we lose on arable,
　Then bungalows will pay.

　　All concrete sheds . . . etc.

　　　　　　John Betjeman

                    th guy drivin round in

                th vankouvr city pound
                truck is giving me
                sum strange
                looks
                    so i
                barkd at
                him

                        bill bissett

The Democratic Judge

In Los Angeles, before the judge who examines people
Trying to become citizens of the United States
Came an Italian restaurant keeper. After grave prepara-
    tions
Hindered, though, by his ignorance of the new language
In the test he replied to the question:
What is the 8th Amendment? falteringly:
1492. Since the law demands that applicants know the
    language
He was refused. Returning
After three months spent on further studies
Yet hindered still by ignorance of the new language
He was confronted this time with the question: Who was
The victorious general in the Civil War? His answer was:

                        12

1492. (Given amiably, in a loud voice.) Sent away again
And returning a third time, he answered
A third question: For how long a term are our Presidents
    elected?
Once more with: 1492. Now
The judge, who liked the man, realized that he could not
Learn the new language, asked him
How he earned his living and was told: by hard work.
    And so
At his fourth appearance the judge gave him the question:
When
Was America discovered? And on the strength of his
    correctly answering
1492, he was granted his citizenship.

Bertolt Brecht

the longer i write poems for you
the shorter they become.

Pamela Brown

You want to change the world.
You settle for changing your mind.
You end up changing your underwear.

You want to be a singer in the band.
You'd settle for singing in the bath.
You end up in a tube car, moaning along to your Walk-
man, hitting three notes out of five and changing key
every two bars.

Dr Kit Bryson and Jean-Luc Legris (extract)

There was a young lady named Bright
Whose speed was far faster than light.
  She set out one day
  In a relative way,
And returned home the previous night.

Arthur Buller

she had more friends
than you could fit
into the back of a truck

that's why she didn't mind
leaving them parked
on a cliff edge

while she went
for a stroll
with the brake in her pocket

Joanne Burns

On Midas's Art

Midas, they say, possessed the art of old,
Of turning whatsoe'er he touch'd to gold;
This modern statesmen can reverse with ease;
Touch them with gold, they'll turn to what you please.

Sir John Byrom

Earwigs

for Mona Simpson

Your delicious-looking rum cake, covered with
almonds, was hand-carried to my door
this morning. The driver parked at the foot
of the hill, and climbed the steep path.
Nothing else moved in that frozen landscape.
It was cold inside and out. I signed
for it, thanked him, went back in.
Where I stripped off the heavy tape, tore
the staples from the bag, and inside
found the canister you'd filled with cake.
I scratched adhesive from the lid.
Prised it open. Folded back the aluminum foil.
To catch the first whiff of that sweetness!

It was then the earwig appeared
from the moist depths. An earwig
stuffed on your cake. Drunk
from it. He went over the side of the can.
Scurried wildly across the table to take
refuge in the fruit bowl. I didn't kill it.
Not then. Filled as I was with conflicting
feelings. Disgust, of course. But
amazement. Even admiration. This creature
that'd just made a 3,000-mile, overnight trip
by air, surrounded by cake, shaved almonds,
and the overpowering odor of rum. Carried
then in a truck over a mountain road and
packed uphill in freezing weather to a house

overlooking the Pacific Ocean. An earwig.
I'll let him live, I thought. What's one more,
or less, in the world? This one's special,
maybe. Blessings on its strange head.
I lifted the cake from its foil wrapping
and three more earwigs went over the side
of the can! For a minute I was so taken
aback I didn't know if I should kill them,
or what. Then rage seized me, and
I plastered them. Crushed the life from them
before any could get away. It was a massacre.
While I was at it, I found and destroyed
the other one utterly.
I was just beginning when it was all over.
I'm saying I could have gone on and on,
rending them. If it's true
that man is wolf to man, what can mere earwigs
expect when bloodlust is up?

I sat down, trying to quieten my heart.
Breath rushing from my nose. I looked
around the table, slowly. Ready
for anything. Mona, I'm sorry to say this,
but I couldn't eat any of your cake.
I've put it away for later, maybe.
Anyway, thanks. You're sweet to remember
me out here alone this winter.
Living alone.
Like an animal, I think.

Raymond Carver

18

Slickness

You
Think
You're slick
I says to him
You
Think
You're tough
Go ahead
Go head
Hit me
Hit me
Hit me
And the ass-hole
He hit me

Michael Casey

Nostalgia

daddy daddy
                    cried the child
what did you do
in the war?

well my son
            said daddy
            who had fought no wars
            but for the usual one
i entered school
became educated
began a fine career
became partner
   in a firm of child manufacturers
built a family
   and a cosy home
and
since then
i have been
slowly strangling
your mother
with it.

Iain Chapman
Lancaster Boys' School, Leicester

The trouble with some women is they get all excited about nothing – and then marry him.

Cher

Reported Missing

Can you give me a precise description?
Said the policeman. Her lips, I told him,
Were soft. Could you give me, he said, pencil
Raised, a metaphor? Soft as an open mouth,
I said. Were there any noticeable
Peculiarities? he asked. Her hair hung
Heavily, I said. Any particular
Colour? he said. I told him I could recall
Little but its distinctive scent. What do
You mean, he asked, by distinctive? It had
The smell of a woman's hair, I said. Where
Were you? he asked. Closer than I am to
Anyone at present, I said; level with

Her mouth, level with her eyes. Her eyes?
He said. What about her eyes? There were two,
I said, both black. It has been established,
He said, that eyes cannot, outside common
Usage, be black; are you implying that
Violence was used? Only the gentle
Hammer blow of her kisses, the scent
Of her breath, the . . .   Quite, said the policeman,
Standing. But I regret that we know of
No one answering to such a description.

Barry Cole

track suit

two-tone stretch nylon yellow stripes on navy blue
i got a brand new track suit i got the old one too
i got the old one too

i got a new track suit
i wear it every day
keeps me cool and casual
i wore it yesterday
i wore it yesterday

i got a new track suit
i wear it everywhere
track me down to the training ground
maybe i'll be there
maybe i'll be there

wearing the brand new track suit
medicine ball to boot
knee pads an airline bag
and the overall smell of brut
the overall smell of fruit

expert eyes have scrutinized
and scientists agree
one track suit would suffice
but you're better off with three
you're better off with three

two-tone stretch nylon yellow stripes on navy blue
i got a brand new track suit i got the old one too
i got the old 1 . . . 2

John Cooper Clarke

From June to December

1 *Prelude*

It wouldn't be a good idea
To let him stay.
When they knew each other better –
Not today.
But she put on her new black knickers
Anyway.

2 *A Serious Person*

I can tell you're a serious person
And I know from the way you talk
That what goes on inside your head
Is pure as the whitest chalk.

It's nice to meet serious people
And hear them explain their views:
Your concern for the rights of women
Is especially welcome news.

I'm sure you'd never exploit one;
I expect you'd rather be dead;
I'm thoroughly convinced of it –
Now can we go to bed?

Wendy Cope (extract)

Eat More

'Eat more fruit!' the slogans say,
　'More fish, more beef, more bread!'
But I'm on Unemployment pay
　My third year now, and wed.

And so I wonder when I'll see
　The slogan when I pass,
The only one that would suit me –
　'Eat More Bloody Grass!'

Joe Corrie

there are so many tictoc
clocks everywhere telling people
what toctic time it is for
tictic instance five toc minutes toc
past six tic

Spring is not regulated and does
not get out of order nor do
its hands a little jerking move
over numbers slowly

                    we do not
wind it up it has no weights
springs wheels inside of
its slender self no indeed dear
nothing of the kind.

(So, when kiss Spring comes
we'll kiss each kiss other on kiss the kiss
lips because tic clocks toc don't make
a toctic difference
to kisskiss you and to
kiss me)

                        e. e. cummings

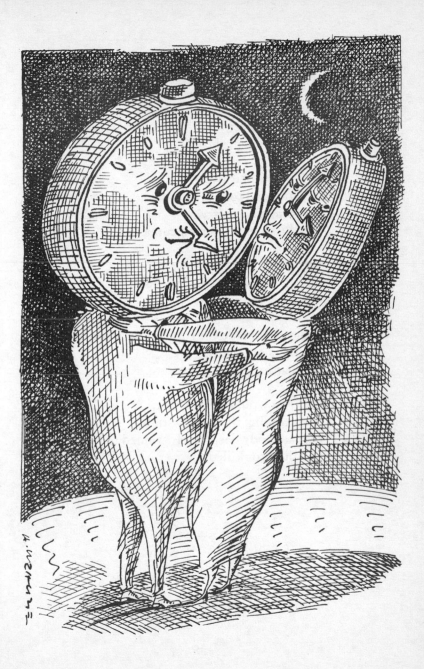

War Memorials 1914–18

Some fell, the inscriptions say,
but did they trip
or were they pushed?

Some lost their lives.
You do tend to lose things
in a foreign country,
but this does seem a bit careless.

Some gave their lives, we're told,
which was certainly generous,
– perhaps, to a fault.

Some even made the supreme sacrifice,
so others assure us,
on their behalf.

But, you would never think,
from reading these memorials,
that anybody desperately wanted to live,
and then got killed.

Bob Dixon

Here lies the mother of children seven,
Four on earth and three in Heaven.
The three in Heaven preferring rather
To be with Mother then stay with Father.

J. S. Drennan

Madman

Every child has a madman on their street:
The only trouble about *our* madman is that he's our
    father.

Paul Durcan

Broadminded

Some of my best friends are white boys.
When I meet 'em,
I treat 'em
just the same as if they was people.

Ray Durem

The moon people
On the dark side of the moon
Are biding their time.
They are curious
But waiting.
They have spotted the
American flag
We left
On the bright side of the moon.
They will come out and
Welcome us
When the coast is clear.
We are waiting, too,
As is our custom,
For the people from the dark side to appear
So
We can
Bomb the shit out of them.
After all,
They are the dark people.

William Eastlake

Sho Nuff

Cold soft drinks
quenched my thirst
one hot and humid July day
after a cool drive
to a mountain store.
Seems like every woman
in the place
had on halter tops
displaying their expensive tans.
There were two women
standing in front of me
at the checkout counter.
One said to the other,
'You must be a lady of leisure,
just look at your beautiful tan.'
Then the other woman responded,
'No, you must be a lady of leisure,
yours is much darker than mine.'
A tall dark and handsome Black dude
standing behind me
whispering down my Black back
s
   a
     i
       d
'Sister, if those two
are ladies of leisure,
you must surely be
a lady of royalty.'
And in a modest tone, I replied,
'SHO NUFF?'

Nilene O. A. Foxworth

Definition

A dog
that dies
and that knows
that it dies
like a dog

and that can say
that it knows
that it dies
like a dog
is a man

Erich Fried
(extract from 'A Dog's Chance')

When asked his opinion of Western Civilization, Mahatma
Gandhi said:
  'I think it would be a good idea.'

Mr Jones

'There's been an accident!' they said,
'Your servant's cut in half; he's dead!'
'Indeed!' said Mr Jones, 'and please
Send me the half that's got my keys.'

Harry Graham

He Had a Dream

I wonder
what
he thought
in that flashing fleeting
pain-filled moment
when
he realized
that
'Turn the other cheek'
won't work
when you been
slapped
by
a .30-30 slug?

Sam Greenlee

Three Poems for Women

1

This is a poem for a woman doing dishes.
This is a poem for a woman doing dishes.
It must be repeated.
It must be repeated,
again and again,
again and again,
because the woman doing dishes
because the woman doing dishes
has trouble hearing
has trouble hearing.

2

And this is another poem for a woman
cleaning the floor
who cannot hear at all.
Let us have a moment of silence
for the woman who cleans the floor.

3

And here is one more poem
for the woman at home
with children.
You never see her at night.
Stare at an empty space and imagine her there,
the woman with children
because she cannot be here to speak
for herself,
and listen
to what you think
she might say.

Susan Griffin

Strange But True

The insectivorous four-fingered sloth mates once every
twelve years. The mating takes from three to four months
and results in the male sloth having to take out a mortgage
on a terraced house in Guatemala while he waits.

Mike Harding

English Literature – GCE

Two dozen pupils
Dissect the set texts
Relentless hands
Ripping apart the delicate flowers
Petal by petal
To learn
How to understand beauty

Savitri Hensman

Impossibilities to His Friend

My faithful friend, if you can see
The Fruit to grow up, or the Tree:
If you can see the colour come
Into the blushing Peare, or Plum:
If you can see the water grow
To cakes of Ice, or flakes of Snow:
If you can see, that drop of raine
Lost in the wild sea, once againe:
If you can see, how Dreams do creep
Into the Brain by easie sleep:
Then there is hope that you may see
Her love me once, who now hates me.

Robert Herrick

What is a Canary?

Hippolyta O'Hara
would like to own
a mare called Bella.

But where would she keep her,
she lives in a housing estate,
no mares named Bella allowed.

Hippolyta O'Hara
would like to own
a minotaur called Harry.

But where would she keep him,
she lives in a housing estate,
no minotaurs named Harry allowed.

Hippolyta O'Hara
would like to own
a crocodile called Leonard.

But where would she keep him,
she lives in a housing estate,
no crocodiles named Leonard allowed.

Hippolyta O'Hara
would like to own
a canary called Dominico,
but the cat would eat him.

'What about the housing estate?'

A canary is a canary
in a housing estate
or in a bishop's house.

The cat is the problem.

Rita Ann Higgins

Brief Reflection on Death

Many people act
as if they hadn't been born yet. Meanwhile, however,
William Burroughs, asked by a student
if he believed in life after death,
replied:
– And how do you know you haven't died yet?

Miroslav Holub

Brief Thoughts on Maps

Albert Szent-Gyorgyi, who knew a lot about maps
   according to which life is on its way somewhere or
      other,
   told us this story from the war
   due to which history is on its way somewhere or other:

The young lieutenant of a small Hungarian detachment
     in the Alps
   sent a reconnaissance unit out into the icy wasteland.
   It began to snow
   immediately, snowed for two days and the unit
   did not return. The lieutenant suffered: he had
     despatched
   his own people to death.

But the third day the unit came back.
   Where had they been? How had they made their way?
   Yes, they said, we considered ourselves
   lost and waited for the end. And then one of us
   found a map in his pocket. That calmed us down.
   We pitched camp, lasted out the snowstorm and then
     with the map
   we discovered our bearings.
   And here we are.

The lieutenant borrowed this remarkable map
   and had a good look at it. It was not a map of the Alps
   but of the Pyrenees.

Goodbye for now.

                            Miroslav Holub

i once addressed
the cows and sheep
but it never got home
and they stayed asleep

i enjoyed myself at first
was witty and intelligent
but after a while i just mumbled
to save us all the embarrassment
of not knowin what i meant

Keith Horn

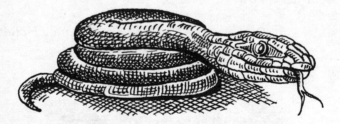

A weak-eyed adder known as Alf
Would curl up on the pantry shelf
And ogle, with the greatest hope,
A coiled-up piece of two-inch rope.

Wilbur G. Howcroft

50—50

I'm all alone in this world, she said,
Ain't got nobody to share my bed,
Ain't got nobody to hold my hand –
The truth of the matter's
I ain't got no man.

Big Boy opened his mouth and said,
Trouble with you is
You ain't got no head!
If you had a head and used your mind
You could have *me* with you
All the time.

She answered, Babe, what must I do?

He said, Share your bed –
And your money, too.

Langston Hughes

Final Curve

When you turn the corner
And you run into *yourself*
Then you know that you have turned
All the corners that are left.

Langston Hughes

Untitled

I can't face work.

I'll turn my back on it.

I turn my back on it.

I've turned my back on it.

Jeltje

I'm starting to wonder what my folks were up to at my age
that makes them so doggoned suspicious of me all the time.

Margaret Blair Johnstone

JILL   I'm upset you are upset
JACK I'm not upset
JILL   I'm upset that you're not upset that I'm upset
       you're upset
JACK I'm upset that you're upset that I'm not upset that
       you're upset that I'm upset, when I'm not.

R. D. Laing (extract)

DOCTOR   How are you?

The patient points to a tracheotomy tube in his neck

DOCTOR   I'm sorry

Realizing the patient can't speak
the doctor takes a pad and pencil and writes

HOW ARE YOU?

and hands pad and pencil to the patient for his reply

The patient takes the pad and pencil and writes

I'M NOT DEAF

R. D. Laing

Family Planning

my mum said that babies
always come from storks
my friend says they're from something
which sounds a bit like 'forks'
i think she's wrong though
but i do know what stops them altogether
it's . . . er . . . um . . er . . . oh yeh . . . corks

Fran Landsman

Middle-Class Children

Another curious thing about the English middle classes
Is how they hate their children.
Those under fifty, and more still, those under forty
They instinctively hate their own children
Once they've got them.

At the same time, they take the greatest possible care of
    them
– Nurses, doctors, proper food, hygiene, schools, all that –
The greatest possible *care* –
And they hate them.

They seem to feel the children a ghastly limitation
– But for these children I should be free –
Free what for, nobody knows. But free!
– Awfully sorry, dear, but I can't come because of the
    children.

The children, of course, know that they are cared for
And disliked.
There is no means of really deceiving a child.

So they accept covered dislike as the normal feeling
    between people.
And superficial attention and care and fulfilment of duty
As normal activity
They may even, one day, discover simple affection as a
    great discovery.

                                        D. H. Lawrence

Tourists

There is nothing to look at any more,
everything has been seen to death.

D. H. Lawrence

Me Aunty Connie

They made cakes at Carson's.
Enormously sticky ones.
With dollops of cream on top,
Jam tarts and doughnuts
Fancy éclairs,
All made at Carson's,
Me Aunty worked at Carson's,
On the cream button.
She put the dollop on the cake
As it passed along the conveyor belt.
She'd been there fifteen years
Then she was promoted
To Senior Cream Dolloper.
It carried responsibility,
And extra buttons.
She had to ensure
No cakes were eaten.
It was instant dismissal at Carson's
To eat a cake.

Laughing and talking
Was also forbidden.
If she'd stayed another fifteen years,
She'd have been promoted again
To the packing machine
What puts the cakes in boxes,
To take them to the shops.
But she didn't stay.
She was offered a higher paid job.
And on her last day,
She dolloped the wrong cakes.
And the Chelsea buns
Went through with cream on them,
While the gâteaus went without.
And the foreman blew his whistle
And stopped production.
The emergency light went on
And the manager came down.
Everyone was laughing and talking.
When he asked her why she did it,
She said because she wanted to.
Course she got dismissal instantly.
But she didn't care.
On the way out,
She picked up a cake
And ate it in front of him.
Everyone at Carson's
Knows me Aunty Connie.

Terry Lee

'The sheep and the wolf
   are not agreed upon a definition
   of the word liberty.'

Abraham Lincoln

Pearls

Dad gave me a string of pearls for my birthday.
They aren't real pearls but they look real.
They came nested in deep, deep blue velvet
  in a hinged box with a silvery lid.
His sister had some like them when she was my age.
She was thrilled.
He thought I'd really like them.
I said I did.

I love the box.

Jean Little

Eve

Let's face it
Eden was a bore
nothing to do
but walk naked in the sun
make love
and talk
but no one had any problems
to speak of
nothing to read
a swim
or lunch might seem special
even afternoon tea wasn't invented
nor wine

a nap might be a highlight
no radio
perhaps they sang a bit
but as yet no one had made up
many songs

and after the honey moon
wouldn't they be bored
walking and talking
with never a worry in the world
they didn't need to invent an atom
or prove the existence of God

no it had to end
Eve showed she was the bright one
bored witless by Adam
no work
and eternal bliss
she saw her chance
they say the snake tempted her to it
don't believe it
she bit because she hungered
to know
the clever thing
she wasn't kicked out
she walked out

Kate Llewellyn

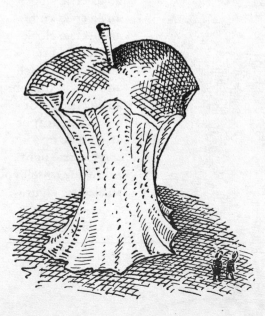

Madam
I have sold you
an electric plug
an electric torch
an electric blanket
an electric bell
an electric cooker
an electric kettle
an electric fan
an electric iron
an electric drier
an electric mixer
an electric washer
an electric peeler
an electric sweeper
an electric mower
an electric singer
an electric knife
an electric clock
an electric fire
an electric switch
an electric toothbrush
an electric razor
an electric teapot
an electric eye
and electric light.
Allow me to sell you
an electric chair.

Christopher Logue

Poem to Help Unemployment

the smell
of freshly peeled prawns
on crinkly crisp lettuce
on freshly buttered brown bread

in slices
in summer
in silence

is like

the smell
of freshly cut grass
on cropped cool lawns
on a Monday evening

in another road
in another suburb
in another town

and what is this poem doing
to help unemployment you ask –
about as much as the Government . . .

Liz Loxley

Archy is Shocked

Archy is a cockroach, who types poems to 'the boss' by jumping up and banging his head on one key at a time.

speaking of shocking things
as so many people are these days
i noted an incident
in a subway train recently
that made my blood run cold
a dignified looking
gentleman with a long
brown beard
in an absent minded manner
suddenly reached up and
pulled his own left eye
from the socket and ate it

the consternation in the car
may be magined
people drew away from him
on all sides women screamed and
fainted in a moment every one
but the guard and myself
were huddled in the end of the car
looking at the dignified
gentleman with terror
the guard was sweating
with excitement but he stood
his ground sir said the guard
you cannot intimidate me

nor can you mystify me
i am a wise boid
you sir are a glass eater
and that was a glass eye
to the devil with a country
where people can t mind their own
business said the dignified
gentleman i am not a glass eater
if you must know and that was not
a glass eye it was a pickled onion
can not a man eat pickled
onions in this community
without exciting remark
the curse of this nation
is the number of meddlesome
matties
who are forever attempting
to restrict the liberty
of the individual i suppose
the next thing will be a law
on the statute books prohibiting
the consumption of pickled onions
and with another curse
he passed from the train
which had just then drawn up
beside
a station and went out
of my life for ever

              archy

Don Marquis

Goodbye

He said
goodbye.
I shuffled
my feet
and kept a close
watch on my
shoes.
He was talking
I was listening
but he probably
thought I was
not
because I never
even lifted my
head.
I didn't want him
to see
the mess mascara
makes when it
runs.

Carol-Anne Marsh

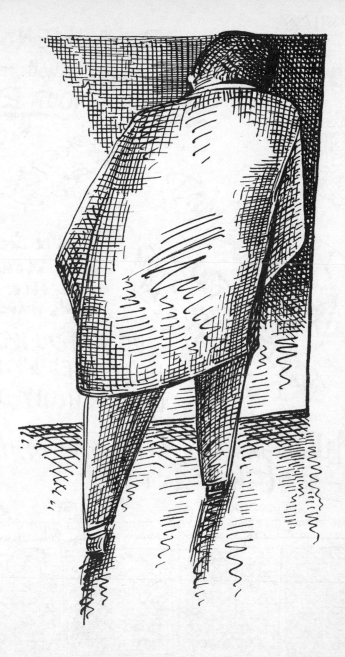

AVOID the END OF THE YEAR RUSH — FAIL YOUR EXAMS NOW!

EARN CASH IN YOUR SPARE TIME.. BLACKMAIL YOUR FRIENDS

DO NOT ADJUST YOUR MIND, THERE IS A FAULT IN REALITY

If you're feeling run down, take the cars number

DO AS YOU WOULD BE DONE BY & YOU'LL BE WELL & TRULY DONE

An Englishman's home is his castle — so let him clean it.

Autopsy's a Dying Art

8 out of every 10 people write with a ball-point pen... what do the other two do with it?

The days of good ENGLISH has went

I'm so unlucky, I even get caught writing on toilet wa

BE REALISTIC – –DEMAND THE IMPOSSIBLE

It begins when you sink into his arms and ends with your arms in his sink

A WOMAN'S WORK IS NEVER DONE BY MEN

Fire Guard

My wife bought a fire guard for the living room.
Seems a nice sort of chap.

Roger McGough

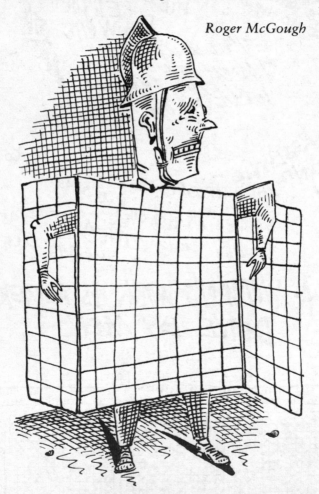

Celia Celia

When I am sad and weary
When I think all hope has gone
When I walk along High Holborn
I think of you with nothing on

Adrian Mitchell

Most people ignore most poetry
because
most poetry ignores most people

Adrian Mitchell

Marilyn Monroe was once asked by a reporter if she really
had nothing on when she posed for nude photographs early
on in her career.
  'Oh no,' said Marilyn, 'I had the radio on.'

All Things Dull and Ugly

All things dull and ugly
All creatures short and squat
All things rude and nasty
The Lord God made the lot.

Each little snake that poisons
Each little wasp that stings
He made their brutish venom
He made their horrid wings.

All things sick and cancerous
All evil great and small
All things foul and dangerous
The Lord God made them all.

Each nasty little hornet
Each beastly little squid
Who made the spiky urchin,
Who made the sharks? He did.

All things scabbed and ulcerous
All pox both great and small
Putrid, foul and gangrenous,
The Lord God made them all.

Amen.

Monty Python

No Say

He says what and what I have to do – to be – to live
He doesn't even listen to me – I must do what
He says
He says I'm wasting my time wanting to be a ballerina
He says there's no future in it for any Black girl
He says   I'm to be a nurse
He says   That's all Black girls are good for.
He says   I must come out him house – if me nor gwan
              listen!
He says   I day-dream too much – But that's all I can do
              I dream of being Odette in *Swan Lake*
He says   I'm too fool for anything
He says   He's my father   I come under his rule.

He says   'Me never bin with a gal so black'
He says   He likes nurses though
He says   I should feel lucky to be with him considering
              he can have any girl
              light skin–red skin–white skin–indian hair
He says   I can't even grind my hips
He says   He's wasting his time
              I think I love him, so I hold on to him.
He says   'It's time me breed yu'
              I can't stand the pain
He says   'Yu lucky it's a boy pickney or me woulda gone'
He says   He's my man

He says   He's hungry – haven't I cooked yet
He says   If I've ironed his clothes he's going out

He says   How can I tell him what time to come home
He says   His white friends don't have hassles at home
He says   He's tired of hearing my voice
             I tried to please him only he doesn't realize
He says   Why get a Saturday job – I'm there to keep him
He says   Just because I've wasted my life – Don't blame him
             Pain can't bear   No escape
He says   He can understand why his father left
He says   He's my son – Not a senseless object

He says – He says – He says   I say – Nothing

Millie Murray

My Black Triangle

My black triangle
sandwiched
between the geography
of my thighs

is a bermuda
of tiny atoms
forever seizing
and releasing
the world

My black triangle
is so rich
that it flows over
on to the dry crotch
of the world

My black triangle
is black light
sitting on the threshold
of the world

overlooking my deep-pink
probabilities

and though
it spares a thought
for history
my black triangle
has spread beyond history
beyond the dry fears of parch-ri-archy

spreading and growing
trusting and flowing
my black triangle
carries the seal of approval
of my deepest self

Grace Nichols

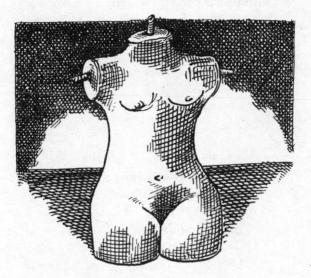

Running Shoes (Guide to Technical Terms)

Impact cushion ~ *small piece of foam rubber.*
Heel dampener ~ *small piece of foam rubber.*
Arch deflector ~ *small piece of foam rubber.*
Reflex insole ~ *small piece of foam rubber.*

Nigel

Life & Trousers

I've tried wearing a belt
I've even tried wearing braces,
I've tried track-suit trousers
with waists pre-elasticated,
but somehow I can never quite manage
to evade that simple truth,
life is just one long struggle
to keep your trousers up.

Andy P.

By the time you swear you're his,
    Shivering and sighing,
And he vows his passion is
    Infinite, undying –
Lady make a note of this:
    One of you is lying.

Dorothy Parker

In America
the medicine looks so good
I want to get ill
and try it.

Tom Pickard

Spic take the broom
and sweep the place
till you make it look
cleaner than heaven
Spic take the mop
and baptize the floor
with soap and water
Spic the garbage can
looks like your salary
make it look like
my salary immediately
Spic I feel hungry
run faster than the speed
of light and get me
a tailored made sandwich
Spic skip your lunch today
for coming late yesterday
Spic I is feeling bored
amuse me with your
broken english humor
Spic the floor is sinning
again do your thing
with the salvation broom
Spic the windows are blind
restore their vision
Spic you have five minutes
to make ten deliveries
Spic stick your tongue out
I want to mail a letter
Spic say goodnight
to your employer he is
exhausted from looking
at you work so hard

Pedro Pietri

Evolution

'Some men are very wicked!' my Gran said
while looking at a monkey in the zoo.
His spectacles of flesh and blue behind
reminded her of someone she once knew.

Fiona Pitt-Kethley

Epigram

engraved on the collar of a dog which I gave to his Royal
Highness Frederick Prince of Wales

> I am his Highness' dog at Kew
> Pray tell me, sir, whose dog are you?

Alexander Pope

Better You Should Learn Wen Do

Men protect women, a man once told me indignantly.
Sure,
some do.
Who do they protect them from?
Other women?
Children?
Wild rutabagas?*
Rampaging rabbits?

Helen Potrebenko

* A kind of swede.

The Starved Man

The starved man has always been a popular figure: those familiar eyes huge with suffering, bigger than his belly, his mouth set grim in the sadness. We have always watched the travels of the starved man. The starved man and friends shot one by one in the back of the head, blown over into Cambodian graves. How well he dies, that man – pulled under by the sharks – his old act with the napalm, running screaming into the jungle. No one has ever died in so many places. The starved man goes to India. The starved man in Ethiopia. The adventures of the starved man in Uganda. How the starved man ate dirt. How he was tortured in Chile. The starved man goes to Haiti. No one has ever died as often as the starved man, yet somehow he manages to keep on starving. One day he will be recognized for this great talent of his. One day he will get an award. Ladies and gentlemen, a man you're all familiar with, my good friend, the starved man.

Robert Priest

Proverb from the Prophet of Palermo

It makes no difference if you're rich or poor – if your nose runs and your feet smell, you're built upside down.

Hustlers

Beggars
cockroach our city
Politicians
in their Mercedes
whizz by in luxury

As long
as one man
has no shirt
and his MP
has two . . .
Count me out
of any Party!

Cecil Rajendra

Song of Bali

Because we believe in industry,
and are convinced we can make money
from our art and scenery,
we have decided to turn Bali into a tourist resort.

Well then,
let's not kid ourselves about what we're doing
when we open Bali to tourists.
After all, jets exist,
airlines need passengers,
and passengers need places to go.
The airlines can compete
to process leisure
and family holidays.

We will shrink Bali,
its art, culture and beauty,
and sell it to the tourists,
wrapped in tinsel.

Jets fly over the forests of Brazil,
past Badui mountain settlements,
appearing in the most unlikely places,
swifter than dreams,
bringing culture shock.

This is a different sort of oppression.
It came so quickly we were taken by surprise.
It came so cunningly we were powerless.

And while we were still dazed,
jet-planes came out of our dreams,
with new forms of financial domination:
hotels serving steak and Coca-Cola;
airports; highways; and sightseers.

'Oh, honey, look!
Look at the natives!
He's climbing that palm tree like a monkey!
Isn't he fantastic! Take his photograph!'

*

'Watch out! Don't touch his hand!
Just smile and say hello.
See – his hand's filthy.
He might have lice.'

*

'My God, they're so innocent.
The women don't even cover their breasts.
Look, John, what magnificent breasts.
And look at this pair. Wonderful!
The people are so free and spontaneous.
I wish I could be like that . . .
OK! OK! . . . I was only joking.
I know you hate it when I don't wear my bra.
All right John, stop complaining!
Stand next to her, dear,
and I'll take your picture.
Ah! Fabulous!'

W. S. Rendra

Epitaph on Charles II

Here lies our Sovereign Lord the King,
    Whose word no man relies on,
Who never said a foolish thing,
    Nor ever did a wise one.

John Wilmot, Earl of Rochester

Lamentations

I found him in the guard-room at the Base.
From the blind darkness I had heard his crying
And blundered in. With puzzled, patient face
A sergeant watched him; it was no good trying
To stop it; for he howled and beat his chest.
And, all because his brother had gone west,
Raved at the bleeding war; his rampant grief
Moaned, shouted, sobbed, and choked, while he was
    kneeling
Half-naked on the floor. In my belief
Such men have lost all patriotic feeling.

Siegfried Sassoon

Rodger

Rodger Mcarthy Mcarthy Mcdoodle
Ninth-generation pedigree poodle
Crufts Supreme Champion once
Runner-up twice
13 shields and 14 cups
Is vet's-clinic-check-upped twice a week
Sleek coat
Shiny nose
'Cos Mummy knows best
And Mummy knows
That whilst Rodger glows with canine health
Money won from Doggy Shows
Grows
Wealth accumulates
Rodger's worth his weight in gold
but

Rodger got RABID

Rodger went MAD

Sad to relate that man's-best-mate
Turns nasty when the virus strikes
Come here Rodger!
Mummy said
Rodger bit off Mummy's head.

Seething Wells

Miriam

So great was my joy
when I received your letter
that on reading it the first time
I didn't realize
that in it you had written
that you didn't love me.

Modesto Silva

The Past

People who are always praising the past
And especially the times of faith as best
Ought to go and live in the Middle Ages
And be burnt at the stake as witches and sages.

Stevie Smith

Two Old Women

The two of us sit in the doorway,
chatting about our children and grandchildren.
We sink happily
into our oldwomanhood.

Like two spoons
sinking
into a bowl of hot porridge.

Anna 'Swir'

Noise

When I play
my records
(at full volume,
in stereo)
I have to
close all
the windows.

I can't stand
the noise
of the birds
outside
in the trees.

Steve Turner

Bertha's Wish

I wish that I didn't have freckles on my face.
I wish that my stomach went in instead of out.
I wish that he would stand on top of the tallest building
    and shout,
'I love you, Amanda.'

One more wish: I wish my name was Amanda.

Judith Viorst

Mississippi Winter IV

My father and mother both
used to warn me
that 'a whistling woman and a crowing
hen would surely come to
no good end.' And perhaps I should
have listened to them.
But even at the time I knew
that though my end probably might
not
be good
I must whistle
like a woman undaunted
until I reached it.

Alice Walker

I'm Really Very Fond

I'm really very fond of you,
he said.

I don't like fond.
It sounds like something
you would tell a dog.

Give me love,
or nothing.

Throw your fond in a pond,
I said.

But what I felt for him
was also warm, frisky,
moist-mouthed,
eager,
and could swim away

if forced to do so.

Alice Walker

Little Red Riding Hood

I always had such a good time, good time, good time girl.
Each and every day from morning to night. Each and every
twenty-four hours I wanted to wake up, wake up. I was so
lively, so livewire tense, such a highly pitched little. I was
red, so red so red. I was a tomato. I was on the lookout for
the wolf. Want some sweeties, mister? I bought a red dress
myself. I bought the wolf. Want some sweeties, mister? I
bought a red dress for myself. I bought a hood for myself.
Get me a hood. I bought a knife.

Ania Walwicz

Greatest Love of All

The greatest
love of all –
to love me!
to love you is
not so great
after all!

Mbeke Waseme

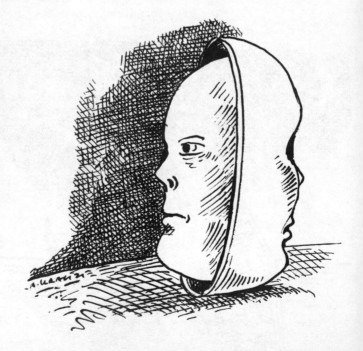

We Sat Talking

We sat talking
all night
about our
beautiful female
friends.

You wanted to
test my jealousy,
My 'devotion' to
you.
Speaking of long
legs, while mine
are short
and of nice
figures, while
I hated mine.

Did you ever think
that the other
woman could be
my lover as well
as yours –
Obviously not!

Mbeke Waseme

Who Wants to Know?

What do you suffer from?

- ☐ country & western
- ☐ health
- ☐ evolution

How often do you speak?

- ☐ 3–6 yrs
- ☐ 7–10 yrs
- ☐ 11–15 yrs
- ☐ 16–18 yrs

How would you describe your upbringing?

- ☐ every day
- ☐ several times a week
- ☐ seldom

How much schooling have you completed?

- ☐ don't no

Your income:

- ☐ almost every night
- ☐ a few times a week

Your religion:

- ☐ above average
- ☐ below average
- ☐ athletic

Where do you go?

- ☐ the sooner the better
- ☐ usually

How intelligent do you consider yourself?

- ☐ it varies
- ☐ it's not for me

Jim Wheat (extract)

Classifieds

● **SLEEP WITH THE STARS!**
Stuff your pillows with hair clippings from your favorite celebrities. Recommended by several customers.

● **HEALINGS BY MAIL!** Send us your ailments. No disease too small. Complete cure by return mail. Disease returned if not satisfied.

Jim Wheat (extract)

Here We Go
by Chelsea Supporters Club

1st Verse:	*Here we go*
	Here we go
	Here we go
	Here we go
	Here we go
	Here we go
	Here we go
	Here we go
	Here we go
	Here we go
	HERE WE GO!
2nd Verse:	*Here we go*
(*Fortissimo*)	*Here we go*
	Here we go
	Here we go
	Here we go
	Here we go*
	Here we go
	Here we go
	Here we go
	Here we go
	Here we go
	HERE WE GO!

(Repeat 1st verse till
final whistle)

* Some versions omit this line.

Who Dares Wins Comedy Team

Shelley Winters once revealed that her ex-husband Vittorio Gassman 'used to grab me in his arms, hold me close – and tell me how wonderful he was.'

Down With Fanatics!

If I had my way with violent men
I'd simmer them in oil,
I'd fill a pot with bitumen
And bring them to the boil.
I'd execrate the terrorist
And those who harbour him,
And if I weren't a moralist
I'd tear them limb from limb.

Fanatics are an evil breed
Whom decent men should shun;
I'd like to flog them till they bleed,
Yes, every mother's son,
I'd like to tie them to a board
And let them taste the cat,
While giving praise, oh thank the Lord,
That I am not like that.

For we should love the human kind,
As Jesus taught us to,
And those who don't should be struck blind
And beaten black and blue;
I'd like to roast them in a grill
And listen to them shriek,
Then break them on the wheel until
They turned the other cheek.

Roger Woddis

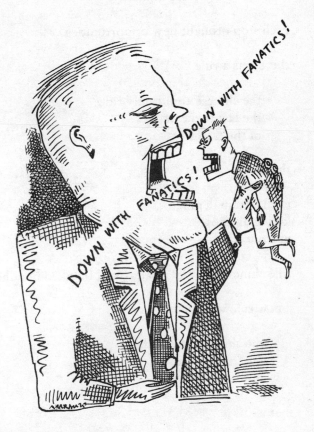

Equal Opportunity

in early canada
when railways were highways

each stop brought new opportunities

there was a rule

    the chinese could only ride
    the last two cars
    of the trains

that is

until a train derailed
killing all those
in front

(the chinese erected an altar and thanked buddha)

a new rule was made

    the chinese must ride
    the front two cars
    of the trains

that is

until another accident
claimed everyone
in the back

(the chinese erected an altar and thanked buddha)

after much debate
common sense prevailed

the chinese are now allowed
to sit anywhere
on any train

Jim Wong-Chu

Mirror Mirror

People keep asking where I come from
says my son.
Trouble is   I'm american on the inside
                and oriental on the outside

    No Doug
    Turn that outside in
    THIS is what American looks like.

                        Mitsuye Yamada

Two Strings to a Bow

I don't want the one that I don't want to know
    That I want the one that I want:
But the one that I want now wants me to go
    And give up the one I don't want.
Why I don't want the one that I don't want to know
    That I want the one that I want,
Is if I miss the one that I want (don't you know)
    I might want the one I don't want.

                        Anon.

How We Met

I was on the train
going to Loftus Road
to see qpr against Arsenal
On the train I saw this boy
on his own
I went up to him
and said 'Are you going to this match?'
he said, 'Yes.'
So I asked him his name.
He said, 'Frank.'
He asked me what team do I
support,
so I said, 'Arsenal.'
Then he punched me in the face
and ran off.

By a fourth-year boy in a
North London Comprehensive

If all the trains at Clapham Jctn
Were suddenly to cease to fctn
The people waiting in the stn
Would never reach their destintn

Anon.

Here
Lies
Lester Moore
Four Slugs
From a 44
No Les
No Moore

Here lies the body of
SAMUEL YOUNG
who came here and died
for the benefit of his health,

Ventnor, Isle of Wight

Here lies my adviser, Dr Sim,
And those he healed – near him.

In Grimsby Parish Church, Humberside

She lived with her husband
50 years
And died in the confident hope
of a better life.

*On a grave in Easingwold
Church, Yorkshire*

To the Moon

Oh Moon, when I look on thy beautiful face,
Careering along through the boundaries of space,
The thought has quite frequently come to my mind,
If ever I'll gaze on thy glorious behind.

Anon.

Acknowledgements

The editor and publishers gratefully acknowledge permission to reproduce copyright poems in this book:

'Stereotype' by John Agard from *Mangoes and Bullets* (Pluto Press), reprinted by permission of Caroline Sheldon Literary Agency and the author; 'Prison Reform' by Pat Arrowsmith from *Themes No. 8*, reprinted by permission of the Communist Party; 'Radio Rap' by Attila the Stockbroker from *Rants*, reprinted by permission of Unwin Hyman Ltd; 'Note on Intellectuals' by W. H. Auden from *Collected Poems*, reprinted by permission of Faber & Faber Ltd; 'Girls Can We Educate We Dads?' by James Berry from *When I Dance*, copyright © 1988, reprinted by permission of Hamish Hamilton; 'Harvest Hymn' by John Betjeman from *Collected Poems*, reprinted by permission of John Murray Publishers Ltd; 'th guy drivin round in' by bill bissett from *Selected Poems*, copyright © 1980, reprinted by permission of Talon Books Ltd; 'The Democratic Judge' by Bertolt Brecht, translated by Michael Hamburger from *Poems 1913–1956*, reprinted by permission of Methuen, London; 'You Want to Change the World' by Dr Kit Bryson and Jean-Luc Legris from *You Want, You'd Settle For, You Get*, copyright © 1986, reprinted by permission of Michael O'Mara Books; 'Earwigs' by Raymond Carver from *Ultramarine*, reprinted by permission of International Creative Management; 'Nostalgia' by Iain Chapman from *ITV English Programme Poetry Competition 1982*, reprinted by permission of the author; 'Reported Missing' by Barry Cole from *The Visitors*, reprinted by permission of Methuen, London; 'track suit' by John Cooper Clarke from *Ten Years in an Open-Necked Shirt*, reprinted by permission of Century Hutchinson Ltd; 'From June to December' by Wendy Cope from *Making Cocoa for Kingsley Amis*, reprinted by permission of Faber & Faber Ltd; 'Eat More' by Joe Corrie, reprinted by permission of Independent Labour Publications; 'there are so many tictoc' by e. e. cummings from *Etcetera*, reprinted by permission of Liveright Publishing Corporation, New York, and Grafton Books, a division of William Collins and Sons Co. Ltd; 'War Memorials 1914–18' by Bob Dixon from *Agitpoems*, reprinted by permission of the author; 'Madman' by Paul Durcan from *Jesus and Angela*, reprinted by permission of The Blackstaff Press; 'Broadminded' by Ray Durem from *Take No Prisoners*, copyright © 1971, London Heritage Series No. 17, reprinted by permission of Paul Breman Ltd; 'The moon people' by William Eastlake from *A Child's Garden of Verses for the Revolution*, copyright © 1970, reprinted by permission of William Eastlake; 'Sho Nuff' by Nilene O. A. Foxworth from *Bury Me in Africa*, reprinted by permission of Mambo Press; 'Definition' by Erich Fried (extract from 'A Dog's Chance') from *On Pain of Seeing*, reprinted by permission of André Deutsch Ltd; 'He Had a Dream' by Sam Greenlee from *Ammunition!*, reprinted by permission of Bogle L'Ouverture; 'Three Poems for Women' by Susan Griffin from *In the Pink* published by Harper & Row, reprinted by permission of the author; 'Strange But True' by Mike Harding from *The Unluckiest Man in the World*, reprinted by permission of Robson Books Ltd; 'English Literature – GCE' by Savitri Hensman from *Flood at the Door*, reprinted by permission of Centerprise Trust Ltd and the author; 'What is a Canary?' by Rita Ann Higgins from *Goddess on the Mervue Bus*, 1987, reprinted by permission of Salmon Publishing; 'Brief Reflection on Death' by Miroslav Holub from *On the Contrary*, translated by Ewald Osers, reprinted by permission of Bloodaxe

(Penguin Modern Classics), reprinted by permission of James MacGibbon, the executor of the author's Estate; 'Noise' by Steve Turner from *Up to Date*, reprinted by permission of Hodder & Stoughton Ltd; 'Bertha's Wish' by Judith Viorst from *If I Were in Charge of the World and Other Worries*, copyright © 1981 Judith Viorst, reprinted by permission of Atheneum Publishers, an imprint of Macmillan Publishing Company and Lescher & Lescher, N.Y.; 'Mississippi Winter IV' and 'I'm Really Very Fond' by Alice Walker from *Horses Make a Landscape More Beautiful* (The Women's Press), reprinted by permission of David Higham Associates Ltd; 'Little Red Riding Hood' by Ania Walwicz from *Writing* (Rigmarole 1982), reprinted by permission of the author; 'Greatest Love of All' and 'We Sat Talking' by Mbeke Waseme (formerly Sharon Bell) from *Exploring All of Me* (The Bookplace), reprinted by permission of the author; 'Who Wants to Know?' and 'Classifieds' by Jim Wheat from *Shouting in a Vacuum* (Nonzense, 1986), reprinted by permission of the author; 'Here We Go' by *Who Dares Wins* Comedy Team from *Who Dares Wins*, copyright © Neonglow Ltd, 1985, reprinted by permission of London Management; 'Down With Fanatics!' by Roger Woddis from *God's Worried*, reprinted by permission of the *New Statesman*; 'Equal Opportunity' by Jim Wong-Chu from *Chinatown Ghosts* 1986, reprinted by permission of Pulp Press Books, Canada; 'How We Met' by a fourth-year boy in a North London Comprehensive, reprinted by permission of André Deutsch Ltd; 'Here Lies Lester Moore' reprinted by permission of Pan Books.

Every effort has been made to trace copyright holders, but in a few cases this has proved impossible. The editor and publishers apologize for these cases of unwilling copyright transgression and would like to hear from any copyright holders not acknowledged.

Index of First Lines

A dog   36
A weak-eyed adder known as Alf   46
Albert Szent-Gyorgyi, who knew a lot about maps   44
All things dull and ugly   70
Another curious thing about the English middle classes   52

Because we believe in industry   83
Beggars   82
By the time you swear you're his   76

Can you give me a precise description   22
Cold soft drinks   34

Dad gave me a string of pearls for my birthday   57
daddy daddy   20
DOCTOR: How are you   50

'Eat more fruit!' the slogans say   27
Every child has a madman on their street   31

He said   64
He says what and what I have to do – to be – to live   72
Healings by mail   98
Here lies a poor woman who always was tired   4
Here lies Lester Moore   106
Here lies my adviser, Dr Sim   107
Here lies our Sovereign Lord the King   86
Here lies the body of Samuel Young   106
Here lies the mother of children seven   31
Here we go   99
Hippolyta O'Hara   42

I always had such a good time, good time, good time girl   93
I am his Highness' dog at Kew   79

I can't face work   49
I don't want the one that I don't want to know   104
I found him in the guard-room at the Base   86
i once addressed   46
I turned on the radio this afternoon   6
I was on the train   105
I wish that I didn't have freckles on my face   91
I wonder   37
If all the trains at Clapham Jctn   105
If I had my way with violent men   100
I'm a fullblooded   1
I'm all alone in this world, she said   47
I'm really very fond of you   92
I'm starting to wonder   49
Impact cushion ∼ *small piece of foam rubber*   75
In America   76
in early canada   102
In Los Angeles, before the judge who examines people   12
In the bad old days   5
It makes no difference if you're rich or poor   81
It wouldn't be a good idea   26
I've tried wearing a belt   76

JILL   I'm upset you are upset   49

Let's face it   58
Listn the male chauvinist in mi dad   8

Madam   60
Many people act   44
Marilyn Monroe was once asked by a reporter   69
Men protect women, a man once told me indignantly   79
Midas, they say, possessed the art of old   16
Most people ignore most poetry   69
My black triangle   74
My faithful friend, if you can see   41
My father and mother both   91
my mum said that babies   51
My wife bought a fire guard for the living room   68

Oh Moon, when I look on thy beautiful face   108

People keep asking where I come from   104
People who are always praising the past   89

Rodger Mcarthy Mcarthy Mcdoodle   87

she had more friends   15
She lived with her husband 50 years   107
Shelley Winters once revealed   100
Sleep with the stars   98
So great was my joy   88
Some fell, the inscriptions say   30
'Some men are very wicked!' my Gran said   78
Some of my best friends are white boys   32
speaking of shocking things   62
Spic take the broom   77

th guy drivin round in   12
The greatest   94
The insectivorous four-fingered sloth   39
the longer i write poems for you   14
The moon people   33
The sheep and the wolf   56
the smell   61
The starved man has always been a popular figure   80
The trouble with some women   22
The two of us sit in the doorway   89
there are so many tictoc   28
There is nothing to look at any more   54
'There's been an accident!' they said   37
There was a young lady named Bright   14
They made cakes at Carson's   54
This is a poem for a woman doing dishes   38
To the man-in-the-street, who, I'm sorry to say   7
Two dozen pupils   40
two-tone stretch nylon yellow stripes on navy blue   24

We sat talking 95
We spray the fields and scatter 10
What do you suffer from 96
When asked his opinion of Western Civilization 36
When I am sad and weary 69
When I play 90
When you turn the corner 48

You 19
You want to be a singer in the band 14
You want to change the world 14
Your delicious-looking rum cake, covered with 17